Australian Military Slang

A Dictionary

Edited by
David Tuffley

Dedicated to the men and women
of the Australian Defence Force
Past, Present and Future

ISBN-13: 978-1495261688 ISBN-10: 1495261689

Wikipedia is the source of the information in the Introduction.

Original Text:
http://en.wiktionary.org/wiki/Appendix:Australian_English_military_slang#R

Acknowledgements
The editor gratefully acknowledges the contribution of all those men and women
who created this dictionary.

Introduction

Australian Military Slang is a window into the rank and file culture of the Australian Army and to some extent the Navy and Air Force. It is an honest, confronting and often humorous look into a culture that most civilians never experience.

Australian military culture has its origins in the traditions of the British military, though over more than a century it has evolved into its own distinct culture.

The Australian military has the fundamental values of courage, initiative, respect and comradeship. There is an ethos of courage and toughness built on a foundation of loyalty and fairness. Around the world, the Australian military is respected for its professionalism, integrity, initiative and esprit de corp. Though relative small compared with other countries, the Australian military is known to "punch above its weight" as the old boxing metaphor goes.

Like any military, there is strong hierarchy. Much of the language is concerned with establishing and reinforcing the military hierarchy. It is essential that everyone accepts their place in the hierarchy.

There is hazing implied in the language. A fighting unit depends on each member to withstand the pressure of combat and do their job. Everyone is tested, and tested again. Anyone found wanting is weeded out before they have a chance to get anyone killed.

Background

The men and women of the Australian Defence Force have a colourful language all their own. Full of profanity and wry humour, it has developing over time, taking influences from the broader Australian dialect, as well as the militaries of other nations, principally Britain and the United States with whom Australia has worked most closely over time.

Readers of *Australian Military Slang* are warned that there is much strong language. If you are likely to be offended by this, then you have been made aware. This dictionary makes no judgment on the appropriateness of the language in relation to community standards. It simply documents it as it is. It is worth preserving for posterity.

In recent times, the Chief of the Defence Forces has made it clear that the culture of 'bastardisation' must end. The military has to be able to recruit new members from the community, competing favourably with civilian careers.

The Australian Defence Force (ADF) is the military organisation responsible for the defence of Australia. It is comprised of the *Royal Australian Navy* (RAN), *Australian Army*, *Royal Australian Air Force* (RAAF) plus a several 'tri-service' units.

While the Australian military is relatively small compared to many of its Asian neighbours, it is one of the most technologically advanced militaries in the world, giving it the capability to operate effectively in the Asia-Pacific and beyond.

The *Royal Australian Navy* (RAN) operates around 70 vessels of various sizes, from frigates, submarines, to patrol boats.

There are two parts to the RAN's structure; Fleet Command (operational) and Navy Strategic Command (support).

The *Australian Army* is Australia's military land force. While the Australian Army is principally a light infantry force, it is in the process of being 'hardened and networked' to enable it to conduct higher-intensity operations.

The *Royal Australian Air Force* (RAAF) is the air force branch of the ADF. The RAAF has up to date combat and transport aircraft plus a network of bases in strategic locations across Australia.

A

ACE, spelt ASM, Warrant officer Class 2 of a RAEME unit, Artificer Sergeant Major. "G'day ace, how are ya Sir?"

Ace fuckheads - headquarters in an armoured unit. Comes from the callsigns 9A, 9C, 9E, 9F, 9H. '90s usage. Being the 2ic, Tech. O, LO, SSM and SQMS, respectively.

ACMS - Army Capability Management System - Because entering all your data in three systems isnt enough (ROMAN, PMKeyS, and MILIS). ACMS excels at reversing the pareto principle, that is, instead of 20% of the work accounting for 80% of the assets, ACMS creates 80% of the work to account for less than 20% of the Army's assets.

Adgie - Refers to a RAAF airfield defence guard.

After fives - Refers to the plain black spit polished dress shoe worn by soldiers either with their pollies or after dinner to give their feet a rest from their boots.

Air Base - A RAAF Base as described by the Australian media, Army and Navy personnel. "Today, an Army C130 Hercules was seen landing at Air Base Amberley."

Airy-fairies - Refers to Air Force personnel, usually used by the Army or Navy. Rarely heard these days.

A.J. (A Jay) - Army Jerk. A derogatory term often used by civilians, RAAF and Navy personnel in reference to soldiers in townships with large concentrations of soldiers (particularly Darwin and Townsville). Also often used by soldiers in reference to other soldiers behaving badly in public, for example "He was being a real AJ" or "They were acting like a bunch of real AJ's and giving the rest of us a bad name". As in 'this was written by an A.J....'. Like many derogatory terms, AJ has been "taken back" by the AJs. In other words it's OK for us to say it, but you might get a slap if you say it. *A.J. fade-away - Refers to a soldiers ability to disappear when they are required to do something or attend something "after 1600 hr marridies did the A.J fade-away from the boozer". also refers to the habit of Army personnel to fade away when having a night out, usually in the form of leaving without saying goodbye to the people they are there with. Often used to describe the habit of Army males leaving the females they have been trying to become romantically involved with. As in "Where'd you end up last night, I didn't see you after dinner?" "Yeah I did the old A.J. fade-away"

AJAX Packet - Ajax packets were placed in the front windows of married quarters to indicate to single men that the man of the house was away, AJAX, AJ Away at Exercise. See OMO. See also FAB.

Angel Raper - Air Defence Regiment (Surface-Air Missiles) member, part of the Royal Australian Artillery.

Angry Chook - Army Chinook heavy lift helicopter.

Angry Palm Tree - Army or Navy helicopter.

Angus - A sub-standard ALSFITT (Aircraft Life Support Fitter, RAAF), usually used as derogatory.

Ankles - See Boots. Also a derogatory term for a dishonest soldier. "Ankles, 3ft lower than a cunt."

APC - Armoured personnel carrier.

APC - Arm, pits, and crotch, a type of bath taken in the bush with limited water.

Arc-up - To initiate an engagement against an enemy force with offensive fire. Also to shout at, as in "Sarge arced-up at me for not ironing my DPCUs."

Arse-end Arnold - Used to refer to the person who is guarding the rear in any field patrol formation (typically used by Army).

Arse Ripping - RAN version of a Face Ripping. Also described as 'Getting torn a new one'

Argit short for Arghhh get fucked!

Army appreciation day - Pay day.

AusCam - An abbreviation of Australian camouflage, the standard camouflage pattern on Australian Military equipment.

B

Back-ups - Seconds (when having a meal).

Bagger - Air Force term for a married member living off-base. Refers to brown-bagging meals from home instead of eating in the Mess.

Bagus - From the Indonesian word for good, Bagus (pronounced in an Australian accent as baggis), is used by Indonesian linguists as an alternative for good.

Bait layer - An Army cook. Refers to a person who drops poison meat to kill dingos.

Balder- Refers to a conversation not worth having.

Bang Seat - Ejection seat.

Bang Stick - A rifle.

BANT - Big arse, no tits, an acronym describing an unattractive woman's appearance.

Banjo - Refers to a bacon and egg breakfast roll wrapped in tin foil and delivered in hot boxes typically to troops staying overnight at the range.

Barbecue - After firing weapons at the range, or on exercise, the unit will spend as long as it takes to clean all the weapons. This is called a barbecue. "After we finish here, we're going back to the barracks for a barbecue." "A barbecue! Great! Will there be beer and snags?" "Ha ha ha, no son, it's not that kind of barbecue." Derived from the similar appearance of both a barbecue and a weapon cleaning bath made from a 44-gallon drum that has been cut lengthwise.

Barracks lawyer - A soldier who professes to know everything about military law, who reckons he could have probably got David Hicks out of Gitmo by finding a technicality in his charge sheet.

Bash - To mould a slouch hat / KFF (q.v.) or beret into an acceptable, close-fitting shape.

Bastardisation - An archaic term used in reference to illegal initiations and punishments that often involved putting subordinates or peers in highly irregular situations.

Bat - Masturbation.

Bat cave - Secluded place adorned with or having access to pornographic material. (e.g., assemblage (Sigs Corps). connex, command bunker/pit (Infantry Corps, Engineers Corps), armoured command vehicle (Armoured Corps)). Usually used on long deployments or exercises. In training establishments, also denotes a supposedly secret location where dirty clothing and other contraband is hidden by recruits prior to an inspection.

Battle tranny - Refers to a portable device (cf. transistor radio) used to access FM/AM radio stations (often cammed up by individual soldiers).

BBDA - Back blast danger area a term used when firing shoulder fired rockets such as the M72 or 84mm Carl Gustav. Also used in emails that are sent out that nobody wants anyone else to see "check your BBDA" you would then check your rear for any onlookers

BBPAG - Big Black Plastic Army Gun - refers to the M60 GPMG (in contrast to the LBPAG (M16) and LGPAG (F88))

Bean counter - Refers to anyone that knows the cost of everything and the value of nothing.

Beasting - To Beast means to stand over or monster a subordinate. The expression is more commonly used by officers. For example, He copped a beasting off the Sergeant Major.

Bedpan scraper - medic

Bear - EW Operator. From the location of 7 SIG REGT at Cabarlah, QLD as in Cabarlah Bears

Beer Issue - "Two beers per night perhaps" Refers to the practice of issuing each sailor two beers either on a special occasion or (rarely) when the time can be spared.

Bible - Pornographic magazines.

Bin-A-Raffie - A not so nice prank where members of the Army attached to the Air Force would throw intoxicated airmen in garbage bins and place bets on how long it takes for them to escape. Game first played at RAAF Curtin.

Bird bath - Washing of Aircrft after coming back from a flight over water (salt water), Hygienic activity taken by a soldier in the field to clean body parts, utilising any available resources such as baby wipes or a small basin of water. This action replaces normal daily showering or bathing at home. Also refers to the airfield spray system used to wash salt residue from maritime patrol aircraft.

Bird gunner - Air Defence Regiment (Surface-Air Missiles) member, division of the Royal Australian Artillery.

Bird shit - Officer pips. Older style DPCU had rank slides on the epaulettes, inferring a bird has shit on the officers shoulder.

BJ - Big Juby.

Blade - Descriptive term for an SAS soldier. "He's a blade'. (From the Winged sword/dagger beret badge of the SAS.)

Blair - A waste of Military funds

Black handers - Air Force term for maintenance personnel working on mechanical systems; i.e., those who get their hands dirty (cf. gay traders).

Black hat or Blackhead - Refers to either Armoured Corps personnel (Black Berets) or to non-SAS personnel (who wear very dark blue berets that look black) posted to the SAS regiment.

Black plastic fantastic - slang for the M16 when the SLR and M16 were the common service rifles.

Blanket stacker/blanket counter - a Quartermaster-bloke. Trained to make large stacks of blankets in the Q-store, and to make sure that the blankets stay where they are. Fully aware of the risk of a collapsing stack of blankets, these highly trained warriors have the stealth of a ninja and the reflexes of a cat.

Blowie/blow fly - Refers to Royal Australian Army Medical Corps Environmental Health personnel.

Blow Flow – see Blowies. Also the civilian contractor who removes the contents of a Honey Pot (see below) when latrines are not allowed to be dug.

Blue orchids - Derogatory term for Air Force personnel (used by soldiers and sailors in reference to their preciousness and scarceness). Also a non-derogatory term used to describe RAAF personnel during WW2 due to their Service Dress Uniform appearing more glamorous than that of other Commonwealth Air Forces.

Blues - Navy or Air Force (Blue) Service Dress uniform. Also Blue Suiter or Blue job, a member of the RAAF (not necessarily wearing blues). Army full dress uniform, commonly used at the RMC. Once issued to all ranks from Sergeant upwards.

Blunt - A derogative term to describe anyone deemed not to be at the sharp end (i.e., front-line/operational). Always a favourite of fighter pilots, who believe that pretty much anyone that isn't strapped into a bang seat (q.v.) is a blunt.

Boffin - An Army electronics/communications technician.

Bog/date roll - Toilet paper.

Boggy - Short for bograt, the slang term for a Pilot Officer (the most junior commissioned Air Force Officer rank).

BOHICA - Bend Over, Here It Comes Again. Often heard prior to the delivery of a pineapple (q.v.); i.e., one is about to be lumbered with an unpleasant task.

Bomb up - To be issued or restocked with ammunition, equipment, or stores.

Bongos - In general, equipment; often refers to field equipment, webbing and/or packs carried on the person. Pack up your bongos and get on that truck.

Bookie [Bukie] or Bookoo - Many. As in 'How many rounds do we need?' 'Bookie rounds, Boss' Presumably derived during the Vietnam period from the Indo China French 'Beaucoup'.

Boots - A suck up. Refers to somebody who is so far up somebody else's backside that all that you can see is his/her boots.

Boozer - Pub or Bar on an Army Base; usually a Soldiers' Boozer as distinct from a Sergeants' or Officers' Mess.

Boss - A complimentary term used by soldiers to refer to their immediate superior officer, usually their Platoon Commander, but can be other Officers in their unit, in the chain of command like the Company Commander or Company 2IC (Second in Charge). E.g., Do you know what we're doing today, boss? Implies respect: unpopular and/or incompetent officers remain 'sir' or 'ma'am'. Also used in the British Armed Forces.

Brass - A high ranking officer. Referring to the amount of brass on someone's uniform.

Brass up - To fire a lot of rounds at something.

Brew - Coffee or tea. Usually made in Standard NATO - Milk and 2 sugars.

Bubba - Useless Member of the Australian Air Force, and biggest RAAF Cock alive. See RAAF Cock.

Bucket - As in bucket of shit. An M113 Armoured Personnel Carrier.

Buckets - A-vehicles, tanks, APCs, ASLAVs, or the Royal Australian Armoured Corps in general. This usage is debated and appears to have been invented by a dumb grunt. Fuckin' smartarse buckets, why do we have to walk? (If we carried grunts, there'd be no room for slabs of coke, chocolate, salami, cheese, travel fridges or all the other stuff that the gentlemen of the Cavalry require when roughing it in the field. And we'd have to take our hammocks down. If you wanted to ride, you should have learnt joined up writing).

Bug out - Leave an area.

Bullshit Castle - Headquarters Air Command, Glenbrook, New South Wales.

Bunghole (Bung'ole)- the very popular tinned fruit pudding in the old 10 man rat pack.

Bush Chook - .A member of 2nd/14th Light Horse Regiment (Queensland Mounted Infantry) because of the emu on their Unit Badge.

Bush hat - The floppy hat worn by soldiers in the field or in non-barracks training.

C

Cake and arse party - Semiformal gathering of officers and / or senior NCOs where alcohol and nibblies are enjoyed. And or where an activity is being poorly run with multiple leaders not really doing a good job EG "Who the fuck is running this cake and arse party?"

Can anybody drive a tractor? - See Motorbike licence

Canteen medals - Beer or food stains on the breast of a shirt or jacket.

Cams - Disruptive Pattern Camouflage Uniform (DPCU), working dress for Army and Air Force and worn on exercises/deployment. Also used in the British Armed Forces.

CDF - Chief of Defence Force; also Common Dog F@#k, See Common Dog Fuck.

C-Dubs - Short for CWD, or Combined Working Dress; the obsolete, Hard Yakka-esque dark blue uniform worn by the Air Force as working dress until the turn of the century. Subsequently replaced by DPCU (see Cams).

Cent - a Centurion Armoured Fighting Vehicle.

Chicken strangler - An SAS soldier; refers to ability to live off the land.

Chief Wheelnut - Refers to a Warrant Officer of the Transport Corps.

Civvy - (Pronounced "Siv-ie") The name given by members of the ADF to non-ADF members. Stems from the word civilian

Choco - (Pronounced "Chock-o") A "chocolate soldier". First used in World War 2 to describe CMF units joining the AIF units in the war in Papua New Guinea. Thought to come about when the CMF passed the AIF on the Kokoda Trail, the CMF would give the AIF that they were replacing, chocolates from their ration packs. Many interpretations of the name's origin include the AIF belief they would melt like chocolate in battle or the fact that they were constantly caked in mud. The name has continued on, referring to current Reservists.

Choc-wit - Term for Army Reservist.

Chook – A signals operator. The term comes from the days of Morse code communications, where an operator transmitting a message resembled a chook pecking the ground. 108th Signals Squadron has the famous cartoon chook Foghorn Leghorn as their unit mascot.

Chook on a stick - the cap badge of 2nd Cavalry Regiment, - the 2 Cav cap badge is a wedge tailed eagle carrying a lance in it's talon, with a guidon bearing the word "Courage". Also the term for the American-Australian monument at Russell Offices, Canberra.

Chookie Scrabble - a friendly competition at after work drinks where the prize is a portion of barbecue chicken. The format of the game is thus: The company/squadron retires early on a Friday afternoon (or on sporties) to engage in some inter-rank fraternisation. Beer is drunk. Approx 30 minutes before the mess opens, when everyone is feeling quite hungry and suitably lubricated, a circle is formed and one or two barbecue chickens are produced, removed from their packaging and lobbed onto the floor. A companies worth of hungry soldiers (and it has been rumoured offices and SNCOs at time) race toward the chooks and compete - bodily and aggressively for a portion of chicken.

Clacker - The hand-held firing device for a 'Claymore' anti-personnel weapon. (As distinct from the mild Australian profanity meaning 'anus'.)

Clicker - A member of 2nd Cavalry Regiment. Also any person who is prone to angry and or crazy outburst, "Man that guy is a clicker"

Clicks - A measure of distance for grunts - how many clicks have we come? A click is a KM.

Clinton - Refers to a person with a soft almost fairy like telephone voice.

Cloud puncher – Refers to the Air defence branch of Artillery.

Clubs - Navy PT Instructor, aka Clubswinger. Derived from the Crossed Indian Clubs (from their category badge) used by the RN over 100 years ago as strength training equipment.

Cluster - Short for cluster fuck. A individual that has a tendency to get things wrong. Can also be used to describe the current situation in a negative light. E.g., Exercise Mantail Sword 2005 was an absolute cluster

Clutch Fucker - Transport driver, derogatory term, joking term

Clunge - Artillery term for a woman on the platform.

Cock Holster - Refers to mouth EG, "shut your cock holster"

Cockroach - An Ordnance Corps (Supply) person, also referred to as a 'ROACH'.

Cockroach Farm - Term of endearment for 292 Squadron, RAAF; the training and support unit for the RAAF AP-3C Orion maritime patrol aircraft.

Coffin nail - A cigarette.

Colour, dash and daring- what the gentlemen of the Cavalry bring to war. Without it/them, war would just be a mindless shit-fight amongst grunts.

Combat PJs - Term used to describe cams when well worn in the field. So known because they are never taken off, even when sleeping.

Combat Wombat - Term used to describe infantry soldiers away from home location as they "eat root, shoot and leave". Also a common name for a digger who is rather short and chubby (resembles the shape and size of a wombat).

Comfy Num Num - the affectionate name given to the DPCU 'jacket' issued to Army personnel. Has a softshell type fabric with hardwearing cordura type fabric at the elbows and across the shoulders.

Common Dog Fuck - Term used when describing how easy something "should" be to understand, "A common Dog would know that, Fuck"

Conehead - See "Boffin". Also refers to Airborne Electronics Analyst crew members on AP-3C Orion maritime patrol aircraft.

Crack the sads - To be sad or upset about anything "Johno why you cracking the sads mate?"

Craftie - A private in the corps of Royal Australian Electrical and Mechanical Engineers (RAEME) - short for "Craftsman".

Crap Hat - Name given to the slouch hat or any non Maroon beret by airborn soldiers who wear the beret. Also a derogatory term for a person who is not parra qualified. EG, Cav Black Berets are crap hats.

Cruds - Recruits in training at 1RTB, also can refer to poor quality food EG "This food is crud" or "Dinner was crud"

Crump in - To have a relatively bad landing when parachuting.AKA "Spudding" in.

CSM - Company Sergeant Major, AKA, Cheif Sandwhich Maker, usually out for the RSM's position.

CUNT - A group of two or more officers. Cunt is also widely used in a non-offensive way EG When greeting a mate, "What's going on Cunt, how ya been?"

Cunt Cap or Pencil Case - Term used to describe a RAAF garrison cap.

Cut Lunch Commando - A member of the CMF (Citizens Military Forces), precursor of the current Army Reserve.

Cyclone Training - To be spread out on ones bed as if to be holding down your bed in a cyclone. Term is widely used in the northern parts of Australia, particularly in reference to soldiers shirking away from work to their rooms and getting some quiet sleep. Also used at Kapooka when instructors tear a Recruits room apart like a Cyclone.

Chucking a fergo - To fall out of a unimog and break your back.

D

Dargan - a Senior Non-Commissioned Officer or Warrant Officer in the Army. see Hendo

Delta - female recruits at 1 RTB (now ARTC) as Delta company housed/trained the female recruits (see groundsheet). Also, "to make a Delta (or D)" is to make a decision. "What's your Delta, Sir?"

Delta Romeo - Direct Reflection. As in "your digger is a shit fight, delta romeo"

DiddlyBop - to run under fire or conduct a patrol (Vietnam Era) We took a quick DiddlyBop round the perimeter to see what Charlie was up to.

Digger – A soldier of the rank of private or equivalent in the Australian Army, for example Look after your diggers, Lieutenant. Term comes from the Anzacs.

Diggers Breakfast - Term used for a 'Smoke and coffee' undertaken during morning routine.

DILLIGAF - Does It Look Like I Give A Fuck.

Dirked : To be assigned a task by a superior, it usually not being a task an individual would volunteer to complete. E.g., I've been dirked by the boss to sell Unit T-shirts at our social function. From the Scottish term for a stiletto or dagger : a Dirk. (See also 'Stabbed').

Dirt Dart - A soldier undertaking Army parachuting.

Dish Licker - Term used to describe a member of the Steward Mustering of the RAAF.

Dit - A DVD; i.e., "What's the Dit?".

Dixies - Small aluminium cooking and eating pans used by individuals in the bush.

Dixie-bashing - Washing up pots and pans.

Dobie - A wash, or shower, from the Urdu 'dobie-wallah,' a launderer.

Dobie Dust - Royal Australian Navy term for Laundry powder.

Doc - Medic.

Doe - A name referring to Commandos, usually by the SAS.

Dog and pony show - A painstakingly prepared briefing, usually of little real substance or value, pandering to the whims of a senior officer. Also used to describe having to participate in some sort of display for civilians as a recruiting drive. E.g. 'The boys got stabbed to do a dog and pony at the footy on Friday night.'

Donkey Fucker - Nickname given to soldiers from 1RAR because their Mascot is a Shetland Pony (refer to SEPPIE).

Donga - Term used to describe a sailors room on base.

Doona wrestling - a favourite "sport"; i.e., sleeping. (Doona is an Australian term meaning duvet or quilt).

"What are you doing for sport this arvo?", "I'm doona wrestling." See Cyclone training.

Door kicker - A member of the SAS who is trained in gaining entry by force.

DPCU - Disruptive Pattern Camouflage Uniform. see 'Cams'.

DPNU - Disruptive Pattern Naval Uniform. see 'Cams'.

Drabs - Air Force Tropical Dress which replaces Service Dress (see Blues) in tropical areas.

Draggie - Device for converting noise into lift/thrust. RAAF term of endearment for the now sadly departed Hawker Siddeley HS 748.

Drop shorts – An artillery solider,'Drop shorts' also implied that gunners dropped their rounds onto our grunts rather than the enemy by accident.

Drut - A Backward Turd, A sometimes derogatory, sometimes affectionate description of an army recruit.

DS Solution - The correct answer to a problem. DS Comes from the term 'Directing Staff'

Durries/darts/darbs - A common army term for cigarettes.To smoke is to 'throw darts'.

Duty First - The motto of the Royal Australian Regiment. It is said to refer to mess duty, guard duty, etc.

E

Eating irons - Cutlery (mainly known in the army as KFS - knife, fork and spoon).

EABOD - Eat A Bag Of Dicks

EAD - term used when reminding someone of having been made to do something unpleasant or extremely time consuming and wasteful, ie 'Hey Davo you got stabbed for duty on Saturday, eat a dick!'

EADC - Eat A Dick Cunt

EAD Knyvett - Eat A Dick Knyvett

EADT - Eat A Dick Trent

EKO - Early Knock Off

Elephant gun - L1A1 SLR Self Loading Rifle (not used while the SLR was the main rifle).

Elephant trackers - RAAF security police. A derisive reference to their supposed lack of investigative acumen.

Emu bob - A line of soldiers, under the control of a junior NCO, side by side, almost shoulder to shoulder, walking slowly forwards cleaning up an area, therefore bobbing up and down to pick up litter (usually cigarette butts or brass), which resembles an emu searching for food. Also known as an "Emu Parade".

Enemy Pam - Woman's fashion magazine

EX - Shorthand for an "Exercise" or training mission/deployment.

Extras - extra duties, used as a form of punishment, usually illegally awarded without hearing by NCOs. Can only legally be awarded after a trial by a summary sub-ordinate authority (i.e. OC level officer). But try telling that to your platoon seargent. I dare you.

F

FAB - FAB packets were placed in the front windows of married quarters to indicate to single men that the Man of the house home, FAB, Fucking Arsehole is Back. See also AJAX.

FAC - "Fucking ADFA Cunt", a Royal Military College Term used to describe ADFA (Australian Defence Force Academy) Cadets, or Officers who have previously attended ADFA.

Face ripping - A one-way discussion, usually between a soldier and a superior, where the "face ripper" gets so close that the "face rippee" can see the pores on his forehead. This usually occurs on the drill square or in the CSM's office.

Fagpants - Refers to a company commander from the early 80s who dressed in lovely technicolour pants - peach, crimson, lime civvie daks at all functions. Now refers to metros.

Fake - Referring to a civilian contractor usually working on a RAAF Base. 'That guy's fake.....'

Fang - Food. To eat or in reference to food. For example "Go and get a fang" or to "Fang out".

Fang Farrier - An Army dentist.

Fang Bosun - An RAN dentist.

Farter - Bed or sleeping bag. Normally refers to going to bed, for example "Hit the Farter". Also known as a Fart Sack, or in the RAN as a Rack.

Fatcans or Fat shop - Describes Australian Defence Force Canteens, for example "I'm going to get some food from Fatcans". Probably derives from AAFCANS - the Army Airforce Canteen Service, which used to run military canteens before Frontline.

Fat-truck - Vehicle used to supply hot food and cold drinks to soldiers in the lines. Driven by the "Fat-slut". Also known as the "Gut-truck" and "gut-slut" respectively or "pie-slut".

Fat, dumb and happy – To be complacent or less than vigilant.

Fat pills – Chocolate and lollies (sweets/candy).

Ferret - Beret

F.I.G.J.A.M. - Fuck I'm Good Just Ask Me.

F.I.N.C.L. - A Fucking Idiot No Cunt Likes. (See Also PTE Fry)

Fish head - Maritime patrol aircrew.

Fisty Cuffs - A term used when two soldiers fight over a disagreement, usually at the boozer. "Johnno and Smithy went fisty cuffs last night!"

Fitter and turner - An Army cook. It means "to fit good food into a pot and turn it into sh-t".

Fitted for, not with - Defence equipment can be expensive. In the interest of good economy therefore the Australian Government has developed the practice of purchasing defense equipment that has provision for certain facilities or features, but is not fitted with the afore said facilities or features. For example Guided Missile Frigates, without Guided Missiles. The idea being that should we even need them, we'll have plenty of time to procure them. And plenty of time will be needed, given the prodigiously spectacular lack of anything resembling movement at Russel Offices. The problem with this idea is of course that the enemy has on occasion been known to attack without letting their targets know (reference Blitzkrieg, Pearl Harbour, etc). This is referred to as a "surprise attack", because it is a surprise. The other problem is that we tend to buy equipment from the US, France, the UK, Sweden and other countries in the other hemisphere on the other side of the world. The ships and planes we'd need to import this equipment might not survive the voyage/flight, as they'd need to be escorted by frigates/fighters etc - most of which are fitted for, but not with key systems. To be fair defense has gotten better over the years and this practise is less common that traditionally was the case, but still occurs to some extent.

Flight Lewie - Nickname for Flight Lieutenant, Air Force Junior Officer rank.

Flight Stupid - Term used to describe a RAAF member of the former Flight Steward mustering.

Flogg Off - Spoken abbreviation for Flying Officer (FLGOFF), Air Force Junior Officer rank. Also used in the Army to describe the act of onaism. At least it was in the 90s.

Foreigners - RAAF term for a job done for a mate as a favour or himself, by a specialist in that area such as a RADTECH fixing a mate's stereo or an MTFITT tuning a car. Usually in work time using RAAF facilities and tools. "Hey Dave, could you do a foreigners on my car tomorrow?" See also Rabbit (q.v.).

Fornicatorium - An armoured vehicle with a meeting room incorporated into its design or any office where (f***ed-up) decisions were made.

Four Star Hotel - The accommodation used by Air Force members on exercise whilst Army members reside in dirt pits or tents if lucky.

F.R.E.D - A small device which is a combination of a can opener, a bottle opener and a spoon. Officially named a "Field Ration Eating Device", but more popularly known as a "F--king Ridiculous/Retarded Eating Device". In the Air Force this acronym can also denote a 'F--king Ridiculous Electronic Device'.

Free balling/furring/snaking - Going without underwear. Often done in the field for hygiene and comfort reasons. Known also as "going commando". See also PTE McDonalds Pants

Fridge - What pogues use to keep beverages cool while deployed in the field.

Frontscam - Another common name for the on base canteen monopoly 'Frontline'.

Frozo - Pre-cooked frozen delicacy provided for the enjoyment and nutrition of RAAF aircrew, primarily AP-3C Orion crews.

Fruit salad - Medal ribbons.

Front Bum - Female, also denotes a sad soldier.

FONC - Friend Of No Cunt - An offensive term for anybody who is disruptive and who does not fit in.

FOX - Used in armoured units for the Squadron Sergeant Major

FTA - Fuck the Army

Fucktard found everywhere but mainly 2/4 RAR roll book or a certain P3 maintenance crew.

Fuck yeah Northy! The reply for when someone has a bad idea, or says something stupid.

Fudge factor to inflate and estimation for unexpected events. 'Carry an extra 50 rounds each as our fudge factor ' or 'Carry an extra 50 rounds as fudge '.

Full-track - Term used in place of the rank Corporal.

G

Galah - Slang term for the in-service underslung grenade launcher (officially called a GLA).

Gammas - Go get some sunlight on the upper decks.

Gay traders - Also "Queer traders". Air Force term for electronics technicians and others working on non-mechanical systems (cf. black handers).

G.A.F. - Give A Fuck.

G'arn garn (go and) get fucked, also see Argit

Gaz - Used to describe someone of unparalleled skill. Also used to describe SAS troops.

Gazontopede - An archaic term commonly used by the Army in the '70s and '80s used to describe somebody who was hopelessly uncoordinated in drill.

Gedunk Machine - refers to a soft drink/candy bar dispensing machine.

Get Your Shit In One Sock - Used to tell a soldier who is typically a shit fight to get orginised.

Get This - Used to indicate thugs from the scallop industry. "Get this! Damn those thugs from the scallop industry!"

Giggle-hat - Bush head dress; '80s term that is fading from use.

Giggle-suit - Bush clothes.

Ginger Beers - Term used to describe a member of the Royal Australian Engineers Corps or RAAF flight engineers.

Glenn Munsie - Glenn is a Sportsbet Market Adviser, his name rhymes with onesies (one-ers), to get a brew for oneself only. "Old Glenn Munsie, got himself a brew again".

Go fast - Unit or other baseball cap worn by RAAF members

God Botherer - The Padre or anybody remotely religious. (sometimes called "sky pilots" or "devil dodgers").

Goffa - Term used by the Royal Australian Navy to describe a salute.

Goffer - Soft drink.

Going commando - See "Free Snaking".

Goinker - Somebody who sucks up to people of superior rank. Also known as a rank watcher.

Golf bag - Accessory pouch for the obsolescent AN/PRC-77 manpack radio or the accessories bag used to carry spare barrels cleaning kit and other equipment for a machine gun.

Gomper/Gumpy Bar - A chocolate bar like a Mars bar or Picnic. "Have a goffer and a gomper mate."

Gong - Medal.

Gonk - To sleep. Also Gonking, the act of having a sleep.

Government Fat - Description of military (tax payer funded) exercise or activity which results in a high level of excitement for an individual - ie, "During tonight's attack, be sure to use all remaining blank rounds before the exercise ends and get your Government Fat on!"

Greenie - Nickname for Electronics Technicians and WEEOs in the RAN. Originates from the green band that WEEOs had between the gold bands on their SRI/HRIs.

Grey Green Brown and Oakover - The names used whenever diggers get in trouble with police or the MPs. Made famous by Gra Gra Kennedy in the movie Odd Angry Shot.

Grey Kingswood - Term of endearment used exclusively by crews of the RAAF AP-3C Orion maritime patrol aircraft; a comfortable and reliable means of transport. Previously "grey and white Kingswood" till someone discovered how visible they were through a submarine's periscope.

Grey-Man - A term used to describe a soldier within his unit who is barely noticed by either his peers or his superiors. This is either the result of him having no personality recognizable by human perception or because he is extremely skilled in the art of being ignored for a work party. Can be used either in a derogatory fashion (Oi cunt, have you been there the whole fucking time? You're such a fucking grey-man!), a respectful fashion (Oi cunt, have you been there the whole fucking time? You're such a fucking grey-man!), or a combination of both (Oi cunt, have you been there the whole fucking time? You're such a fucking grey-man!). Very useful skill when not out in the field.

Groundsheet - Derogatory slang for a female soldier. I.e., something you lay on the ground.

Greaser - A vehicle mechanic. AKA VM

Grumpy Old Cunt - Ralph Blewitt

GRUNT - An acronym meaning the same in Australia as it does everywhere else, a negative name for an infantry soldier. Often adopted with pride by the Grunts themselves. (Government Reject Unfit for Normal Training).

Gruntapede - The term Tank drivers use for Dismounted Infantry.

Gucci - A piece of kit that is really good or expensive.

Gun Bunny - An artillery soldier.

Gunny/Gunnie - Air Force term for an armaments fitter. No relation to the US Marine Corps rank of Gunnery Sergeant.

Gun Plumber - A fitter/armourer, usually those attached to armoured units.AKA Tiffie, See Tiffie and Artificer, fitter.

H

Half Screw/Half Track - Term used in place of the rank Lance Corporal. Also see Full Track.

Handbag – A signals operator (archaic usage). The term is derived from the satchel used carry a VHF dipole antenna known as an Antenna Lightweight for either a 'Seventy Seven Set' or its modern equivalents. Particularly applicable to Royal Australian Signals Corps personnel as their corps badge resembles the Interflora symbol. Also used to be used to describe medics whose medical kits looked like handbags and were often carried like a lady carries a handbag.

Handbaggers – Operator Movements, part of the Corp of Transport. RACT soldier, who plans, coordinates, executes, controls and monitors the operational and strategic movement of personnel and equipment of the ADF.

Hard Corps - RAInf, the Royal Australian Infantry Corps. Sgt: What corps are you, dig? Digger: Hard corps, Sergeant.(Some idiot grunt whos never been deployed must have wrote this)(3 RAR)

Harden up - A standard response to whinging or complaining, telling a person to shut up and get on with the job. Often provided in imaginary consumable form; e.g., here's a harden-up pill, have a can of harden-up or "drink some concrete and harden the f..k up!".

Head shed - Headquarters at any unit level.

Healthkeys - Medical data base system that in theory is supposed to make life better for medics but in reality is a tool for blood sucking bean counters and auditors that load up the medical system with even more work.

Heartlidge -A derogative term used for a lack of Heart, Will and or any sign of weakness during moments of mental and or physical discomfort I.e. What Happened to Pte ****? Why did he not finish the 30 K stomp? Is he injured? Nah the weakling cunt just pulled a heartlidge!

Hendo - The biggest Dargan of the Australian Army. See DARGAN

Helicopter pad - A badly bashed (q.v.) beret.

Helo – Army/Navy term for helicopter (pronounced HEE-Lo).

Helicopter piquet - Usually used when in the field, it refers to soldiers shirking away from work by lying down somewhere. From the idea of looking up for approaching helicopters. Similar to Cyclone Training.

Ho Chi Min Shuffle - a slow run designed to conserve energy over long distances. The feet are not lifted very high.

(To get) **Holes In Your T Shirt** - To get shot, usually on a "Two Way Rifle Range".

Honey pot _ A cylindrical galvanized steel receptacle used for defecation out in the field. Usually emptied or replaced by soldiers lance corporal and below.

Hoochie/Hutchie - Individual shelter sheet used in the field. Presumably derived from hooch, a term for a Vietnamese rural dwelling.

Hook in - To perform a task aggressively or with gusto. "Hook in, get your work done and we'll have an early knock off". Army slang from the '60s, '70s, '80s, and '90s.

House on back – To put on ones pack; because soldiers in the field are required to live out of their pack.

Hot box - The large plastic containers which bring fresh rations to Diggers in a field environment, which contains inadequately small portions of cooked vegetables and a small helping of whatever yesterday's leftovers were from the base mess packed into tinfoil trays.

Hurry up and Wait - The repercussions of letting an officer organise an activity. Diggers are normally harassed to get their shit in one sock, only to wait as the PL COMD, OC, CO, and BDE Commander have all added a fudge factor into their planning numbers. Normally results in arriving at a rugby match at 0700 for a 1430 kick off.

Howard Green - An issued Khaki green Wooolen Jumper with material sewn on the elbows Pre - 1992 (DPCU Version issued post 1992). Also a Common name used by soldiers when introduced to a female they just met at a nightclub, knowing they would never see her again (Refer to AJ Fade Away) and (Sam Brown).

I

IFIIK - I'm Fucked If I Know.

J

Jack – To be selfish or to go it alone, for example Don't jack on your mates!, Going Jack, or Stop being jack and give us a hand. The term comes from digger jack...he didn't put in.(PTE FRY)

Jack-up - going on strike (akin to a mutiny but unable to identify ring leaders - comes from the industrial background of the mass armies of the world wars)(potentially archaic)

Jack – A sailor, from the term Jack Tar.

Jackhammers – An elite section of technicians who not only strive to produce airpower but in fact succeed and excel.

Jack Rations - civilian food taken to the field to liven up the issue rations. As in "I'm all right Jack Fuck you" or "don't be jack, let me have one of your goffas".

JAFA - Just Another Fucking Admino (Administration Officer is a RAAF Officer Category).

Jam Shrewsbury - a magical mystical morale biscuit found in ration packs. Often discovered heartbrokenly crushed. Can be used as currency out bush. Golden Rule - Never ever fuck with a mans Jam Shrewsbury.

Jedi – An adjective or noun indicating respect for a colleague's military professionalism. Nick gave us a totally Jedi briefing on the Musorian ORBAT - he's an INT Jedi. A reference to the supernatural warrior caste depicted in a well-known film series.

Jellybean-dispenser – F1 sub-machine gun. Derived from the jelly-bean like appearance of low velocity bullets that may be observed leaving the barrel.

Jellybean-suit - Offensive term for army camouflage used by RAN or RAAF. No longer offensive, now used by Army just to describe their cams.

Jockstrap or Jock - A digger who is renowned for sporting prowess and his inability to go bush, or do his job with his mates.

Jube - A new or inexperienced soldier, thought to be because they are soft and sugar-coated. Phonetically: Jewb, Joob, or Just Out Of Basic

Jubie juice - Fruit flavoured cordial, for example, Have a drink of jubie.

K

Kav - Refers to a person who sleazes out of an activity - like a route march by feigning injury or illness, named after an infamous individual in the BB1. 'He did a Kav and jumped in the safety vehicle.'

Kepi - Refers to a small peaked cap worn by some members of the Royal Australian Armoured Corps often closely resemble those worn by the German Afrika Corps.

KFF - Khaki Fur Felt (Hat). More official term for the Slouch Hat.

KFS - Knife, Fork, and Spoon. A piece of equipment which hosts all three cutlery items.

KFS Course - A six week induction course undertaken by specialist officers who are not required to undertake 18 months training at Duntroon. Named so because pretty much all that can be taught in six weeks is how to use a knife fork and spoon.

Killick - Pronounced Kelleck. Informally denotes the rank of Leading Seaman in the RAN, the word itself describes a type of anchor made from wood and stone and is applied as a result of the rank insignia of a Leading Seaman being a fouled anchor. A Killick is also know as a Leading Hand, or Leader.

King-of-the-Shits - a WO1, usually the RSM [See also Shit-of-the-Kings].

King Shitter - A recruit at ARTC Kapooka who is charged with overseeing the cleaning of the lines during morning routine (specifically the SALs, or shitters).

Kip - A short sleep or nap.

Koala Bear - Refers to somebody who is generally considered a protected species and useless in the greater scheme of things. Usually accompanied by the phrase "Not to be exported or shot at" was used to refer to 1st Armoured Regt.

Knob Tickler - Anyone who puts shit on 1RAR .

Knock-off Bird - an action where soldiers within a group call "Knock-off!" in a high-pitched voice like a cuckoo clock, usually suggesting that they knock off for the day whilst remaining anonymous.

Knuck - A fighter pilot; short for 'knucklehead'. Also used in US military slang. Also used to denote fighting, ie "going the knuck on that guy".

Klingon - Term used to describe a waring race of aliens in the science fiction series Star Trek, and used to describe a RAAF member attached to a Squadron/formation/unit for a period of time. "Corporal, who are those numpties? Klingon's Sir, from 10 SQN.

L

Laddy - Soldier who is always injured until a sports team is playing.

Lance Jack – Term used in place of the rank Lance Corporal. E.g., We have 3 Corporals and 2 Lance Jacks in this unit. The term comes from a VC winner. Also used in the British Armed Forces.

Lance Propeller – Derogatory Term used in place of the rank Lance Corporal for RAAF personnel.

Legend - A Legend of the regiment - generally over used, but traditionally used to describe characters like Warry George, Richo Richardson and Blue Telford at the Battle School.

Legendary Battalion - They believe they are legends when essentially they're reserve infantry. Leave it to the big boys.

Legend in their own Lunchbox - A person who beats their own drum or has an over inflated opinion of their own abilities. See Squeezers, Fucktards, Legendary Battalion

Leaveapp Looser - Term used to describe a Clerk in the Royal Australian Air Force.

LBPAG - Little Black Plastic Army Gun - refers to the M16 when the SLR and M16 were the common service rifles.(in contrast to the BBPAG (M60) and LGPAG (F88))

LGPAG - Little Green Plastic Army Gun - refers to the F88 Austyer when the SLR and M16 were the common service rifles.(in contrast to the BBPAG (M60) and LBPAG (M16))

Lid - Live-In Divorced and Single. Comes from Soldiers post-Vietnam. Also used to denote a new/ the most junior member of a section, ie 'Limited Intelligence Drone. Or Rhyming slang(for Kid) "Billy Lid" or shortened to Lid, eg "I'm not cleaning the shitters, let the Lids do it".

Linger - Abbreviation of w:Malingering. Also pronounced as Lingering or Lingin. Refers to soldiers faking an injury to get our of certain activities. He's a linger or he's Lingin again (See Kav)

Light Colonel, Half Colonel - Lieutenant Colonel

Limers - Navy term for cordial fruit drink.

Living the Dream - Sarcastic catchphrase used to express dissatisfaction with unpleasant duties.

Lobster - Refers to a Physical Training Instructor, usually meaning "Hard on the outside and head full of sh-t". Also refers to their bright red training uniform.

Love Hearts and Bunny Rabbits - Term used to describe DPCU's due to its camouflage pattern resembling that of love hearts and bunny rabbits.

Luncheon Meat Type 2 - An inedible can of pink stuff issued in some Ratpaks. Do not attempt to eat. Do not attempt to feed it to a dog - dogs won't eat it.

M

Maccas - Chips, crisps, chocolate bars and other food sold in canteens or messes

Maggoty - Short for "maggot bag", meaning a meat pie.

Maggot - A 2 RAR mortarman. Thought to come from Vietnam when after a contact they were found by the CO blind drunk who labelled them maggots.

Makan - Pronounced Muc-Karn. From Bahasa Malaysia for meaning "eat."

Makers - Naval euphemism for an early stand-down from work. Derived from the naval custom of 'make and mend', whereby sailors were allocated 'free' time to repair personal clothing and equipment.

Mango - Term for Army Reservist. Green on the outside, yellow on the inside and too many of them give you the shits.

Mas - Indonesian word for "brother" used by elderly to describe males of younger age or lower status, or by younger men to each other. A term of endearment used by Indonesian linguists as a substitute for "mate".

Meat Bomb - See "Dirt Dart".

Meat Heads - Derogatory term referring to Military Police (well in use before their red berets). Also known to refer to Army Physical Training Instructors (PTIs).

Mike-Mike millimetre; often used to describe 9 mm ammo.

MIMMS - A convoluted computerised materiel management system (Mount Isa Mines). The bane of the existence of RAEME and RASIGS trade personnel.

MILIS - A 400 million dollar system that replaced MIMS and SDSS (Standard Defence Supply System), created to stop the Supply system. Very successful (see sarcasm).

Mog - Referring to an ADF medium transport truck the Mercedes Unimog.

Maggot - Term used for an Army Cook, due to the white working dress uniform they wear.

Morale Vampire - Usually refers to an officer who is highly focussed on his own goals and needs, showing little or no care for the welfare or needs of the soldiers under his command.

Mordor - Canberra, the Australian National Capital and location of Army Headquarters.

Motion thickness - Involuntary erection experienced by male personnel when sitting over the wildly vibrating wheel arch of a Unimog truck. A traveller (q.v.) or travel fat . The sort of pun you find really funny when you're 18 years old.

Motorbike licence - A ruse to get diggers to volunteer for something. Sgt: Has anybody here got a motorbike licence? (Two or three new diggers jump to their feet) "I have Sergeant!" Sgt: Good. Grab these shovels and go dig a latrine. Diggers: What about the motorbike? Sgt: GRAB THOSE SHOVELS AND START DIGGING!

Muppet - an un-coordinated or unintelligent individual. Usually used in terms of "fucking muppet" or "Bloody Muppet". Also an old apprentice Neumonic - "Most Useless Person Pussers Ever Trained"

Muppet-Arms - someone who is either woefully inaccurate or incapable of throwing or carrying objects. Most often heard in grenade throwing when someone doesn't throw the grenade far enough from the bunker.

M&M's - (Medals and Money) A term used to denote those in the RAAF who got a three month non-formation rotation to East Timor, and later other area's of operation (ie, a Flight Sergeant from Defence Personnel Canberra sent to East Timor in 2000 for guard duty) to get their M&Ms.

N

Nard or Ratpack Nard - A turd, particularly one that is layed after subsisting for days or weeks on Ratpacks, usually resembles a log, extremely dense, hard and painful to excrete.

Nard Roll - Toilet Paper.

Navigation Aid - bright blue or yellow potaloos placed in the field, usually located at checkpoints during a nav ex ensuring no one gets lost.

NFI - No fucken' idea. Or No Fucken' Interest. Can be both. You choose.

Nigel - Inhabitant of the area immediately surrounding Butter worth Air Base, Malaysia. Also use to describe Vietnamese during Vietnam conflict; i.e., "Nigel Nog", possibly from the very common Vietnamese family name Ngyuen.

Nog - Vietnamese person (not necessarily enemy). Used during the Vietname conflict. See also 'Nigel'.

Numpty – An individual who just doesn't get it, for example This numpty recruit forgot his boots. Also used in the British Armed Forces. From the Scots, as in, "He's a numpty head" normally used in reference to the English.

O

Off Cut - Nickname for an Officer Cadet, derived from the abbreviation OFFCDT.

Oci Dot - Nickname for an Officer Cadet, derived from the abbreviation OCDT.

O Group - A meeting conducted by a commander where orders are distributed. The shortened form is an 'Owey'.

Old Mate - Any person about whom you speak, for example "Old mate over there isn't working that much" or "Old mate came up and tried to bum a few ciggies off me."

Oncers - RAN slang for tomoto sauce - from something that happens to women "once a month".

OMO-relates to an omo laundry detergent box being placed in a window in a married patch to indicate "Old Man Out" See AJAX & FAB

OP - Shorthand for an "Operation".

On the pill - to get with, smarten up (used in the 1960s and 70s)

One-ers - Naval term for making tea or coffee solely for oneself, without offering to make a cuppa for your mates. A jack (q.v.) practice.

Onesies - Army term for making tea or coffee solely for oneself, without offering to make a brew for your mates. A jack (q.v.) practice. Also referred to as a Glenn Munsie.

Onion - Air force nickname for a P-3 Orion.

Oppo - A friend or comrade, usually also in the military.

Oska - The name of an infamous baitlayer in the Big Blue One who was alleged to have organised a long remembered function at the Copper Refinery in Townsville which led to financial and professional losses.

Other enemy - Archaic term for Military Police or Provost, now little used.

Oxygen thief - A person who is so useless that existence deprives the rest of the human race of oxygen. Becoming assosiated with CPL Newman and incompetent officers.

P

Pam - Military doctrine manual

Pams, excitable - Pornographic material. Derived from the army use of the term pamphlet to refer to a training manual.

Pam 19 - War comic. Usually the quarto sized 'Battler Britton' style. So called as there was no Pamphlet numbered 19.

Packed lunch commando - a member of the CMF or Army Reserve.

Paper, scissors, rank - Similar to paper, scissors, rock, however rank always wins.

Passion fingers - A clumsy/incompetent soldier, sailor or airman, i.e. 'everything they touch, they fuck.'

Penguin Swarm - Where soldiers huddle closer together when standing outside in the cold. Often occurs when soldiers return from operations in tropical or desert areas to southern Australia during winter.

Pies and Beers – A play on the term Ginger Beers. Refers to Pioneer specialists from the Royal Australian Infantry Corps who carry out less technically demanding engineering tasks than Royal Australian Engineers Corps personnel.

Pig Battalion - The Seventh Battalion of the Royal Australian Regiment (because the first words spoken to it on parade by its first CO Lt Col. Eric Smith in 1966 at Puckapunyal Barracks was " you're nothing but a bunch of pigs" after a bad weekend by most ranks on the turps. As a result, thier mascot is now a pig and adorns thier APCs. They used to own a pig as a mascot but it died after spending years drinking beer and eating bacon, cigarette butts and hotboxes (including the tinfoil container). Much like 7RAR soldiers.

Pig - An officer (within the RAAF, Snorker has become a popular alternative, to avoid confusion with the aircraft).

Pig - An F-111 aircraft. Also an Australian RAAF nickname given to SAAF's Piaggio "Albatross" aircraft.

Pig pen - The officer's mess, Or a F-111 Hanger.

Pineapple - A term used to describe an odious task or command, delivered by a Sergeant or above. Akin to having a pineapple jammed up one's arse. To get 'pineappled' or receive a pineapple.

Pissaphone - A conical metal funnel partially stuck into the ground for soldiers to urinate into. It looks a bit like a five foot long loud hailer, but those who use it for that purpose usually regret doing so.

Pixie shirt/greens - 'Old school' name for the 'tropical' jungle green field uniform, distinguished by pockets on the shirt sleeves and slanted chest pockets. Refers to its tight-fitting cut compared to earlier versions; i.e., only a pixie could fit into it comfortably. Replaced by DPCU (q.v.) from the late 1980s onwards.

Plastic fantastic - Steyr F88 rifle, standard assault rifle for Australian infantry. Not used as often now, but was once popular when the rifle was first introduced due to the (for the time) revolutionary use of plastics in construction.

Pleasure fingers - A technical or mechanical challenged RAAFie who "fucks whatever he/she touches."

PMKeyS - The succubus Defence computer database that consumes 60% of all human endeavour. A staff officer's wet dream, it is particularly useful for creating nice pie charts to impress the CO (see also: dog and pony show).

Pollard - Term of endearment for a retired Grunt who has lost most of their hair and has trouble drinking Shirley Temples.

Pollies – The polyester dress, for example Iron your pollies, dig!. The term comes from the material they are made from (polyester). Also known as polys.

POETS Day - Friday - Piss Off Early Tomorrows Saturday

Pongo - A derogatory name for a soldier. "Where the army goes, the pong goes."

PONTI - "Person Of No Tactical Importance" A derogatory term used to describe rear echelon staff

Pogo or Poag – A soldier not involved in combat. Usually in protected areas well behind the front lines. Comes from POAG (Posted On A Garrison) or POGO (Posted on garrison operations). Also the term was used in the Vietnam era as rhyming slang for 'Pogo Stick' (rhyming with 'Prick'). This term is often used by any soldier against any other soldier or group who he/she perceives as living an easier life than their own. Can also take the form "pogue" (Person Of Greater Use Elsewhere), same spelling as used for "Person Other than Grunt".

Poof Mat - Insulating sleeping mat used out field.

POR - Privilege of Rank

POS - "Piece Of Shit" Originally conceived for a particular cadet whilst he was undergoing training, now commonly used to describe someone who is a social retard who makes everyone cringe when they open their mouth. Also used when someone does something stupid, annoying or Jack "You are such a POS". POS acronym can be extended if need be (i.e. Friend of POS = FPOS).

Prove - Raising your hand on command - e.g. "All those with a Mog driver's licence - prove!".

Popey - Term used by clerks when problems occur with simple filing or lost documents. Named after a grossly incompetent Lance Corpral clerk.

PTE FRY - Soldier with no concern for his mates welfare, especially on ops".

Pucka Tucka F-cka - The Army Cooks at Puckapunyal.

Pusser - A sailor, also used in the Royal Navy; derivative of 'purser'. Originally used to describe just the supply branch. (Pussers rum was issued to the British Navy)

Q

Q - Quartermaster - An officer who has the enviable job of making sure that the Q-store is always full of every kind of stuff ever invented, and making sure that those dirty diggers don't get any of if because they will break it for sure. Delegates these tasks to ordinary Q-blokes.

Q-blokes / Q-wallah / Quey - People who work in the Q-store.

Q-store - Quartermaster's Store - A large building full of stacks of every kind of stuff you could ever want or need. If you ask for any of it, you will be told: "Sorry mate, I've only got one left and somebody else might want it." You may be offered a few consolation tins of Luncheon Meat Type 2, or if you're really lucky, Ham And Egg In A Can.

Quarmbie - Used by the Army, it refers to a highly uncoordinated person lacking in motor skills. Usually in relation to drill or weapon handling. E.g., A Drill Quarmbie

Queer Trader - An Avionics Technician. Boffin on aircraft(generally Army) Not actually a job; More a sexual preference.

R

RAAF Cock - An RAAF member who displays a lack of healthy disdain for RAAF values. also shows a disgusting level of enthusiasm in regards to his employment and RAAF assets. example

Bubba: "gee! did you see that hornet doing a full AB takeoff!? how cool was that?!" Ryan: "Pfft Hornets are gay! your such a RAAF Cock!"

Rabbit - RAN term for a job done for a mate as a favour or himself, by a trade specialist in that area such as a technician fixing a mate's stereo or repairing a car. Usually in work time using RAN facilities and tools. "Hey Dave, could you do a rabbit on my car tomorrow?" See also Foreigner

Racing spoon - A large spoon carried by most front line soldiers for use in a group meal or "train smash". The bigger the spoon the more you can get in one go. Usually carried for weeks at a time, and cleaned by wiping it on your cams.

Rack - Term used to describe a sailor's bed on-board a ship. See 'Farter'

Raffie - Used by the Army and RAN to identify Royal Australian Air Force personnel ..."He's a Raffie."

RAAF-nob/Ronnie RAAF - Used to describe those RAAF personnel who take their job too seriously, examples include: MSI's (Military Skills Instructors, formally known as GSI's, General Skills Instructors) and WOD's (Warrant Officer Discipline).

Rank Skank - A female soldier who sleeps her way through the Chain of Command.

Ration Assassin - An Army cook.

Rat-catcher - Common and affectionate term for Royal Australian Air Force's Environmental Health members or hygienists.

Ratpak - Refering to an ADF ration pack.

Redders - Tomato sauce. A tomato sauce stain on one's uniform is a redders medal.

Red Tabs - Referring to Senior Officers in the Army: Colonel and above. They are distinguished by the red tabs worn on their collars.

Resup - a resupply, usually in the field of water, food and ammunition.AKA Replen.

Retread - A soldier that is changing trades. Used while they on course to distinguish them from Initial Employment Trainees.

Reg - (rhymes with "egg") A regular (full-time) soldier.

Regi - To be extremely regimental. E.g. Someone/something who is very down the line and extremely strict, ie '4 field is the regiest unit ever.' or ' Fuck I cant stand the RSM, he is so regi.'

Rick O'Shay - (A.K.A) The Mad Irishman - slang for ricochete.

Rock, The - Common name for Penang used by personnel at Butterworth Air Base, Malaysia

Rock show - Used to describe a poorly planned or managed activity..."That exercise was a complete Rock show" or "This is fast turning into a Rock show"

Rocking horse shit - Term to describe something that is rare.

Rodeney - A bloke who spells with a stutter, once again, more than likely associated with 1 RAR"

Rong Hill - The name used to describe officers who cannot navigate.

Roofing Nail - The modern, wide-brimmed hat for wearing out bush. Also used to describe such hats when still new- ie the brim is still straight.

Rooted - To be very very tired or when someting is broken. "God I'm rooted after that pack march" and or "That Land Rover is rooted after Johno drove it"

RQMS - Old warrant officer storeman who is convinced he is smarter than everyone and has all the answers to questions you didn't even ask.

ROP - Restriction Of Privileges. A type of punishment handed to a person who has been found guilty of a military offence (a defaulter).

RP - A Regimental Policeman. The sycophantic arse-lickers who follow the RSM around, and lap up tasks like drilling defaulters and nailing parade ground markers into the ground. Out of the same stable as a "Meat Head".

R.H.I.P - Stands for "Rank Has Its Privileges", sometimes quoted as "Rank Hath Its Privileges".

Rupert - An Army Officer (from British Army - newly commissioned officer and therefore very inexperienced).

Rum Ration - Term for the daily issue of Grog or Rum the used to be given to sailors, unfortunately they no longer issue rum and it doesn't come daily. See "Beer Issue"

S

Sad-on - To be unhappy. What's up mate? You've had a sad-on all day.

Sads - To whinge, as in Crack the sads.

S.A.L- Shit At Life- A nickname refering to a solider whom fails at everything: "Oi Sal, get over here". Also "showers and latrines" - old skool way of saying bathroom.

Sally Man - A Salvation Army Officer. A term of endearment.

Sam Brown - Leather Belt and shoulder strap worn by Army Officers when wearing polys and their ceremonial swords. Also a Common name used by soldiers when introduced to a female they just met at a nightclub, knowing they would never see her again (Refer to AJ Fade Away) and (Howard Green).

SAS - Special Air Service or when used to describe Army Reservists means 'Saturdays and Sundays'.

Sea Squarie - Navy term for the cloth needed as a result of indulging in self-satisfaction, typically used when in ones rack (bed).

Second To None - The motto of The Second Battalion Royal Australian Regiment (2RAR)

Seppie - 1st Battalion RAR Mascot (Shetland Pony)

Scablifter - A medic.

SCRAN - Term used to refer to food - "Sultanas, Currants, Raisins and Nuts" and "Shit Cooked by the Royal Australian Navy".

Scran-bag - Lost clothing bag. Also used metaphorically to describe a slovenly, disorganised or incompetent sailor: I don't want 'X' on my watch, he/she's a complete scranbag.

Screw - Corporal.

Screws - Another derisive term for RAAF security police. Quick, the screws are coming!

Second Class Ride - what armoured corps soldiers get. Better than a first class walk, which is what crunchies do ('Crunchies' refers to anyone on foot near a moving armoured vehicle, as they make a crunching noise when they get run over).

Sergeants Mess - Where sergeants go to aviod work, talk smack about their troops or sometimes eat... Also a place where RAAF Cocks are in high abundance. - See 'RAAF Cock'.

Seventy-Seven Set - AN/PRC-77 manpack radio.

Shit fight Used to comment on the way a soldier looks, how his/her room looks or how something is turning out; e.g., 'You're a shit fight Gunner Dickson, sort your shit out' or ' This is turning into a shit fight'. Can be upgraded to fuck fight as necessary.

Shit-locker Used to describe a large stomach of a service person; e.g., "Get that dog's eye into your shit locker".

Shit-of-the-Kings - a 2nd Lieutenant. [See also King-of-the-Shits]

Shit pit - A latrine. You'll be digging lots of these if you admit to having a motorbike licence.

Shmooey-Tue - A Vue-Tue filled with pornography.

Short arm parade - Inspection of soldiers' genitals to discover any VD infection.

Show Bags - Someone who is full of shit. Derived from the easter show gimmick bags full of usless crap.

Sig - A private in the Royal Australian Signals corps, for example Sig Smith go to the Q-Store to collect our equipment for the EX. Abbreviation for Signalman.

Singo- Location of the School Of Infantry,Singleton NSW home of the Australian Infantry. So when did you go through Singo mate?

SL(u)R - A name for the L1A1 rifle. It was a Real Man's Weapon... but then again our ancestors lamented the passing of the boomerang & spear.

Skippy Badge - Hat or beret badge insignia for the Royal Australian Regiment (Regular Army Infantry organisation) Skippy for the kangaroo in the centre

Sack - Short for sack of shit. All units have a few

Slouchie or **Slouch Hat** - Unique form of wide brimmed khaki/light brown coloured fur-felt hat worn by

Australian Soldiers with the left brim turned up for ceremonial occasions. A KFF.

S.L.U.G. - slow, lethargic, unco-ordinated, grot. Often used for those who are physically challenged or endemically hopeless.

Smellie - A Short Magazine Lee Enfield rifle .303 (in Australian Service No1 MkIII or its varients in the main) (archaic).

Smock, psychological- a camouflaged nylon rain garment intended for field use, issued from the 60s-early 90s. Provided only psychological protection from the rain.

S.N.A.F.U. - Situation Normal All Fucked Up.

Snake - Term used to refer to Sergeants. Also refers to Naval Police Coxwains in the RAN.

Snake Pit - Term used to refer to the Sergeants Mess. Also shortened to "the pit". E.g., "See you down the pit."

Social Climber - Derogative, used to describe a person who tries to mix and socialise in with higher ranking persons and groups.

Soggy Sao - Equivalent to the British "biscuit race". "SAO" is a brand of cracker biscuit made by Arnotts. First started in the Australian Defence Force by members of 4th Field Regiment.

Sombrero - Refers to the new bush hats which have extremely wide brims. "look at that jube with a sombrero. Get some time up."

Space Cadet - 1). Name for a Staff Cadet(Officer in training) with rank abbreviated as SCDT. 2). An individual who has no idea, 'is off with the stars'.

Spanner - A member of the corps of Royal Australian Electrical and Mechanical Engineers (RAEME).

Spam in a Can - Occupants and crew of an APC or tank. The after effects of being hit by anti-tank weapons.

Spanker - See Hoffrichter or Pollard.

Sparky - An electrician or electronics tech of the RAEME.

Splat-cat - See 'Dirt Dart'.

Splat-cats - 3 RAR

Splice The Mail Brace - Order given by the Queen for the 'Rum Ration' to be doubled, this is only done only rarely done to celebrate occasions such as the birth or marriage of a member of the Royal Family.

Sponge - Term of endearment for Russell Offices, Canberra. Also "The Grey Sponge", "Big Grey Sponge" or "Sponge Factory"

Spook - A name used for RAAF Intelligence Officers: "Yeah, that FLTLT's a spook."

Spring-Butt - Derogatory term for a student, usually staff college, who loves to show the world how much he knows by asking interminable questions of guest lectures at every opportunity, usually preceded by a preamble demonstrating their own exemplory level of knowledge of the subject in question.

Square Peg - Short for "Square Peg Round Hole", See F.O.N.C.

Squashed Moth The aircrew brevet - the 'wings' badge worn on a pilot's uniform. By extension, derogatory slang for aircrew.

Squeezer - A jocular term of derision used to describe another soldier or person who is suspected of malingering (e.g., Old mate is a f#cking squeezer)

SSM - Senior Sandwhich Maker the same as CSM but 2nd in charge of a SQN

Stabbed - To be assigned a task by a superior, it usually not being a task an individual would volunteer to complete. E.g., I've been stabbed by the boss to sell Unit T-shirts at our function.

Standard NATO - Milk and two sugars.

Stars - Infantry sleep under them, RAAF select their accommodation by the rating, Navy claim to navigate using them.

Steamer - A crap.

Stinger - A member of B sqn 3rd/4th Cavalry Regiment.

Subbie - An officer of subaltern rank; i.e., Army Lieutenants, Air Force Pilot/Flying Officers, and Navy Sub-Lieutenants.

Super-grunt a member of the Special Air Service.

Super-Sub-Lieutenant or Super-Sub-Lewie - RAN term used to describe a RAN Commodore as their rank (now sleeve rank) resembles that of a super large Sub-Lieutenant's rank.

S.W.A.T - refers to the reserves. Some Weekends And Tuesdays

SWAT - Students Wanting A Taste refers to gap year members

Sweating like an ADG in a spelling test - To perspire excessively.

SLATTERY - refers to an individual weak in nature and non productive, also a dick (see woftam).

T

Tail-end Charlie a soldier who is bring-up or protecting the rear of a platoon, or formation (same as "Arse-end Arnold").

Tailor mades - Mass-produced cigarettes; i.e., bought as is, as opposed to rolling your own ('rollies').

Tally - RAAF term; originally denoted visual acquisition of an airborne target, but has become frequently used in a bar/nightclub scenario. 'Ya see that brunette in the red dress?' 'Tally.'

Tanker/Tanky - Member of the Armoured Corps.

Tankwit - A Member of 1st Armoured Regiment. Comes from the term "Dimwit" meaning that a crew is locked up inside their Tank and has no idea whats going on around them. "Oh he's a Tankwit"

Target - Naval surface vessel according to submariners and aircrew.

Tazzed - (aka Getting Tazzed) - RAAF officer term for drinking alcohol to excess and throwing up after a big night "you were really Tazzed last night"

Tea and medals - A successful conclusion to an operation. From the British TV series 'Blackadder Goes Forth'.

Tea and Sticky Buns - A one-way conversation during which a wayward member (usually an officer) is reminded of his or her short comings by a senior commander.

Ten That Cunt - a card game played by members of 11PL "ZULUs" of Delta Coy 2RAR

Ter - An Indonesian prefix generally meaning something is the "most" eg. "Terbesar", Besar = big, terbesar = biggest. Ter is used by Indonesian linguists in everyday English to add emphasis to something. eg. "I'm terhungry" or "that chick is terhot."

Terry tuff cunt - Someone who thinks they are tough but are really just try hards, "Hey Mick, check this Terry tuff cunt out"

T.H.E.M. - SAS

The Train - Often a Domestic operation served by at least 3 diggers but usually as many as a young lass can handle in quick succession, i.e., "Did you end up picking that bird up last night?" "Yep, me and the boys ran a train on her, she just couldn't get enough."

Throw Smoke - To throw smoke is to cover a tactical withdrawal from a sticky situation, also to make a strategic withdrawal during a civilian outing with AJs (see also AJ Fadeaway)

(A) **Thick** - An army tradesman who did not serve an army apprenticeship (generally in the days when Army Apprentices School existed)

Throw Down - a enemy weapon held by a section for emergency legal reasons.

TIC - Troops In Contact.

Tiffy - Artificer, a member of the RAEME who works on and repairs Artillery and Tank guns. "My gun is rooted, took it down to the tiffies and they said it will be fixed in 3 to 5 hours"

Tillie - An M548A1 Tracked Load carrier - member of the M113 family used for cargo/resupply duties.

Tink Tink - A member of the army who wears glasses. 'Tink Tink' is the sound of the rounds from the sniper rifle finding their mark, as the the glasses reflect light and draw attention to the wearers location.

TOADs - Army Reserve. Tuesdays Only After Dark.

TOC - Tea or Coffee, refers to self funded canteen of a unit.

Tooth Fairy - A member of the Royal Australian Army Dental Corps.

Train Smash - A meal made by combining any ingredients from one or more rat packs into a pot and heating. Usually eaten by a group.

Training Pam or Training Manual - hard core pornography.

Traveller or travel fat - Used to describe an erection caused by vehicle motion / vibration. Also known as 'motion thickness'.

Trooper Seiko - When you use a watch to do your picquet (preferably not on Ops).

Tubbin - Thumb Up Bum Brain In Neutral.

Trash haulers - Transport aircrew. Often shortened to 'trashies'.

Trashies - Slang for AAFCANS, a RAAF canteen. (Trashies referring to the low quality fried food served there).

Triple Points - An attractive female officer. Derived from the HMAS Success event in 2009.

Trucky - A slang term used for soldiers of The Royal Australian Corps Of Transport.

Truckwit - Used as a derisive term to describe a Transport Corps soldier (by other corps to describe an inept Transport Corp member).

Tubs - A shower.

Tucker fucker - An Army cook. 'Tucker' is an Australian word for food.

Tully - Tully, home of the Field Force Battle School, with the highest rainfall in Australia. Run in the early 80s by a true legend - Warry George Mansford, and with great staff like Blue Telford, Blue Gleeson and some other ring ins. Renouned for the toilet humour, mostly left by depressed poges on their first visit away from their base, e.g. TULLY - Totally Unbelievable Lets Leave Yesterday.

Tupperware - Steyr F88 rifle see Plastic fantastic. Derived from the name of a plastic kitchenware manufacturer (Tupperware is the name of the plastic kitchenware company which also makes the butt group and trigger mech of the rifle).

Turd Burglar - A soldier from 2/4 RAR same as a Poo Pirate , Shirt Lifter or Nugget Puncher.

Turd toucher - A plumber/gasfitter tradesman from the RAE.

Turps - Any form of alcoholic beverage drank to excess.

Turret-head - Member of the Armoured Corps.

Two-way rifle range - The battlefield.

Two-dads - A generic name for someone with a hyphenated surname. I.e., two surnames, therefore two fathers.

Tyre Biter - A term used to describe a driver within the Tranposrt Corps.

U

Uckers - A board game from the Royal Navy, similar to Ludo and thought to have originated in India. [1]

Underwater Panel Beating - See 'Dixie Bashing'.

UNSWR'd - To get completely screwed over regardless of actual successes. The obscuring of results in order to make someone feel spesschal. that result last Saturday got completely UNSWR'd [2]

V

Vege bin - An armoured personnel carrier. Implies that the troops carried in the vehicle are 'vegetables'.

Veggies - Royal Australian Armoured Corps Assault Troopers. Depending on the context the term can be one of endearment or derision.

Veggie Patch - 1 RAR at Lavarack Barracks.

Vue Tue - Pronounced 'viewee toowee'. Refers to a small green plastic folder with clear plastic sleeves for inserting notes and cribs commonly used by the Army. Aussie equivalent of a 'Nirex' (UK) or 'dope book' (USA).

W

WAG - 'Wild Arse Guess'. Usually made by an Officer when "navigating".

Wagtail - Sometimes affectionate term for the "Wagtail" radio due to its long antenna.

Wank booth - A soldier's room on base.

Wanking chariot - A single bed on base.

Wanking spanner - Your prominent hand. E.g., "Stick your wanking spanner in the air if you ....". (Also known as (c__t scratcher").

Warned Out - to be notified of an impending task.

Warry/warrie - A colourful (if somewhat embellished) anecdote about military service 'back in the day'. Usually recited by a senior NCO after a surfeit of alcohol. The best warries eventually transmute into urban legends. Australian equivalent of the USN/USMC term 'sea story'.

Waste of space - A member of the ADF that fulfills a posting that could be better done by a blind and mute primate. Usually fails the basics regarding ADF life, BFAs etc. Commonly throws junk food down their gullet and is a chain smoker yet talks about selection plans.

Wheelbarrow with a... - Used by Army personnel when confronted with a long and/or difficult to pronounce name. E.g. a Corporal at 1 RTB might be calling out the roll and be confronted with the name 'Tsimbouklis', which he would then call out as "wheelbarrow with a 'T'"

Whiskey Tango - A term that refers to a female from another country. White Trash.

White Handers - Air Force term for maintenance personnel working on electrical systems; i.e., those who don't get their hands dirty.

Whore's bath - A quick wash taken in the field with little water- i.e. armpits and crotch.

Willy Foxtrot - The Whimp Factor, Willy Foxtrot. Usually used when someone dogs it from a hard activity - he got a dose of the Willy Foxtrots.

WOFTAM - 'Waste Of Fucking Time And Money'. Once used by Regulars to describe Reservists, but you don't hear it so much these days.

WOMBAT - Waste of military budget and time.

Wombat gun - M79 grenade launcher. More common now is the GLA (Grenade Launcher Attachment) for the in service F88 AUSTEYR.

WRAN - 'Women in the RAN', in past times it was always used as a mark of respect. Depending on context it may still be a mark of respect, or more commonly used to simply designate a group of female sailors without any respect or otherwise implied. Sometimes used to describe a particular female sailor who may be a little promiscuous, with the obvious derogatory connotation that accompanies that lifestyle.

Wreckie mech - An RAEME soldier who operates motor recovery equipment; i.e., a wrecker. Generally NOT very bright. Known as the LEGENDs of DRONG in RAEME. Also known as Bogoligists.

X

Xongabong - refers to the act of using marijuana while on active duty. ie- John got discharged because he was xongabong.

Y

Yowie suit - Heavily camouflaged garments worn by snipers, resembling a mythical creature of the bush. Australian term for a Ghillie suit.

Yardie - Glorified blanket stacker, also able to stack items on lage wooden pallets.

Yarma - Bloody big hill, as in we just patrolled up that f%^&ing big yarma!

Z

Zeds or Zees" to sleep is to "punch out zeds".

Zoom bag - A flying suit.

Notes

Notes

Notes

Notes

_____

_____

_____

_____

_____

_____

_____

_____

_____

_____

_____

_____

_____

_____

Notes

Notes

_____

_____

_____

_____

_____

_____

_____

_____

_____

_____

_____

_____

_____

_____

_____

_____

_____

Notes

_____

_____

_____

_____

_____

_____

_____

_____

_____

_____

_____

_____

_____

_____

Notes

Notes

_____

_____

_____

_____

_____

_____

_____

_____

_____

_____

_____

_____

_____

_____

Notes

Notes

Notes

Notes

Notes

Notes

Notes

_____

_____

_____

_____

_____

_____

_____

_____

_____

_____

_____

_____

_____

_____

_____